SPOKEN
MEDITATION FROM THE HEART

CAUSTEN MEAUX SR.

Copyright © 2022 by Causten Meaux Sr.

All rights reserved. No part of this publication may be reproduced, distributed, or transmitted in any form or by any means, including photocopying, recording, or other electronic or mechanical methods, without the prior written permission of the author, except in the case of brief quotations embodied in critical reviews and certain other noncommercial uses permitted by copyright law.

Printed in the United States of America

ISBN 978-1-952182-88-4 (sc)

ISBN 978-1-952182-89-1 (e)

Published by CAUSTEN MEAUX SR

Author: Causten Meaux Sr

If I could store in a safety vault every second of every day of my life, then at the time to review for my next decision, reboot or retrieve to analyze my next step or decision based on times past, I could avoid setbacks and live every day in a blissful almost perfected life. Imagine, never ill-fated feelings or misguided decisions that would intrude and interrupt the serenity of this blissful existence. Every day I could cry out to the world "look at me, I have all the answers". But life is a progression to an expected end. Every second produces a change. Living cannot be programmed or patterned. Every breathing being was birthed into his own, totally independent of others, all caused by divine design. I have not the power nor the knowledge to take the next step nor the next breath nor even the next thought without the continued aid of my designer. I am not my own. Meticulously was I brought to life. A constant eye and hand is on me. My designer will never leave me alone. He guides me day and night. He strengthens me in my weakest moments. He even heals my hurts. I know not what lies ahead but I am confident in my designer. His design was perfect just for me. My uniqueness pleases him. In Him, my Creator, I move and have my being.

Causten Meaux Sr

Dream Past Your Dreams

How great would it be to reach out and touch those precious and almost mystical dreams of last night! As though perfection and serenity were the main courses, I recall with a sigh of warmth the mere thought of the dream. Shaking my head in despair, I look around and see reality. Settling back into the routine of the life, what was at the moment a feeling of satisfaction vaporizes, and I then go forward with the task of the day. But what if I could go past my dreams? Would that be just a hopeful fantasy, or could I with a determined and realistic effort make my dreams come true?

Alone

    I sit alone to the world with my thoughts. Strategically I silently and internally plan those things: that I desire to become real, tangible, and alive. The communication with myself will either clarify or distort. If I am not careful, I will become entrenched in a vacuum of muddle confusion. Internalizing without true vision can result in unstable actions. Life is lived internally but displayed externally.

Activated Salvation

Looking at the forms of the word action (activated, activation, and active), it defines the need for some measure of energy spent that causes motion. Applied to salvation (the saving grace of God), the mere confessing of faith that Jesus Christ saves us from eternal death does not activate our power to resist temptation. Getting a credit card only reminds us that we have possession of something that is valuable, but only by activation will it give the results for which it was acquired. So it is with our salvation. In order to access the power, action must be taken daily. Consider the three P's: pray without ceasing, persistence in obedience, and patience in all things.

Enjoy Your Freedom or Remain in Prison

How wonderful it is to decide. The cliché "I'm grown and I can make my own decisions" ring loud and clear and true.
However, the reality of life is that no man is an island and man knows not beyond the words that he speaks the outcome of that which has been spoken. The ability to see further than one can see leads to a blind spot. One will remain imprisoned by one's self and unable to break through the surrendering of one's soul to Him who has created. For whom the Lord sets free is free indeed.

My Existence

I didn't choose my existence, but I do choose how to live it both in the flesh and in the spirit.

Life

The fulfillment of life is in the fullness of God. I just want God to fill me!

Direction

    My inability to make the right decisions lies within my sinful nature. Knowingly or unknowingly turning to disobediences renders me incapable of viewing that which lies ahead. Proverbs' instructions reveal God's plan for me to be led and directed through this life: "In all thy ways acknowledge Him and He shall direct your path."

Believing

The power of believing is activated by the spirit.
What spirit is guiding you?
Never pray in desperation. Always pray in faith.

Process

The forward progress of my focus often times will eliminate some of the rough times as I proceed. Understanding and accepting the imperfections of myself will allow a continued movement toward the unaccomplished. There are many stepping stones that will eventually lead to that place of completion. Lest I stop short, the ultimate will never be obtained.

Resounding Voice of Death

I have been assigned to you to complete what is, before you can become what you were created for. I am ever revealing, and I pray your eyes, ears and heart are attentive to my voice. I have given visible signs and wonders so that you may be without excuse or caught off guard. There is no escaping and no compromising. I have been given my assignment, and I too cannot escape. Soon I will be no more. Please do not ignore my voice. Oh, by the way, today is the day of opportunity.
Don't let it pass you by.

The Cycles of Life

At birth, you don't understand that you are in the world. At age ten, you don't know what the world is.
At age twenty, you could care less about the world. At age thirty, you try to conquer the world.
At age forty, you think the world owes you something.
At age fifty, you begin to realize that the world is passing you by.
At age sixty, you start to realize the blessings of being in the world.
At age seventy, you understand that there is a better place. Above age seventy, you long to leave the world because you understand the promises of God, threescore and ten. If I never get to the stage of my life where I long to leave this world, I may be of the world and not just in the world.

My Heart Leaps for Joy

When I begin to meditate on my life and the miracle of life itself, my heart leaps for joy. How many times have I lain down at night, and how many times have I awakened? My heart leaps for joy. To think that in God's omniscience, He chose me and purposed me to live. I have been created for His glory. When He formed me and He looked at His masterpiece, He saw that it was good. Now as I thank Him for what He did just for me, my heart leaps for joy.

I'm Not That Innocent

I look the look of a conqueror.
I walk with the assurance of my direction. I speak with authority and purpose.
My smile is pleasing to the eyes. My stance seems permanent.
So why am I not that innocent?
I struggle daily with things that keep me searching and seeking for some resolve. What is it that will not allow me to spend just one day in total relaxation of thought and action? The more I ponder, the more I wonder.
Then as though some sudden light appears as I think and meditate, there are two of me: Flesh and the Spirit. My flesh has been birthed in sin trying to persuade or sway my spirit. This causes a great divide. So what do I (the spirit) do? I bring to remembrance my Creator, who breathed the breath of life in me and made me a living soul. It was God the Father who gave His only begotten son, Jesus Christ, as a ransom just for me. I am not that innocent, but the Spirit within washes me, with the blood of Jesus, whiter than snow and makes me perfect before the Almighty God. Therefore, I can stand tall, be strong, and let His Spirit overpower and hide my multitude of sins. No, I'm not that innocent but guilty as charged. But I have been saved by grace through faith in Christ Jesus.
Signed, The Redeemed

When It Happens, and It Will

How do you handle the pressures of life when days seem like nights and nights become days? How do you handle the disappointments and rejections? Where do you go when everything you try to do fails? What becomes of a hopeless situation? What do you do when it happens, and it will? Just remember the one who is omnipotent, omniscient, and omnipresent. Is there anything too hard for God?

Sin Was Blocking Me

Stumbling and falling seems to be my plight. Running into roadblocks and dead ends is my daily routine. The harder I try, the less I achieve. It's not fair that others prosper and I struggle. Why is God not seeing and hearing me? It wasn't until I confessed to myself that it was the sin (un-confessed and un-repented) that was blocking me. Then with a sincere heart, I ask God to forgive me. Now barriers in my life have been lifted.

Opinions

     Opinions about scripture is unfounded and non-biblical.
Opinions are based on perception (what I think and how I see) and not truth. Although God has given us the ability to reason and to think, only the Holy Spirit can reveal truth. My opinion, feelings and what I perceive is null and void when it is not revealed and confirmed by the Spirit of God. The Spirit bears witness to Himself. The Bible is the perfect and true Word of God. Acceptance of Truth builds a spiritual sincere heart.

My Pride----His Promise

Do I trust and rest in me, or do I trust and rest in Him?
I want what I want when I want it. He gives me what I need when I need it.
I get restless. He gives me peace.
I get tired. He never slumbers nor sleeps. I get weak. He is omnipotent, all powerful.
I get confused. He settles the troubling mind.
I feel as though the weight of the world is on my shoulders. He holds the whole world in His hand.
I feel so alone. He will never leave nor forsake me. I am so afraid. He has not given me a spirit of fear.
I want so much but can't seem to get but a little. He says, "Seek ye first the Kingdom of God and His Righteousness" and "all" these things will be added.
How do I lose my pride? Be not conformed but be transformed. Present your body as a living sacrifice, wholly acceptable unto God. The Word says to "trust in the Lord totally, with your whole being and lean not to your own understanding."

Blessings in a Denied Prayer

Beyond the knowledge of mortal being, beyond the feelings of mortal man, beyond the desires of the things ahead, beyond the desires for the flesh to be fed lies the infinite wisdom of the Almighty Sovereign God. The Creator knows. "My grace is sufficient for the" (2 Corinthians 12:9).

Conviction

The spirit convicts the soul (the consciousness of man), and the soul condemns the flesh. The soul is in darkness until the spirit gives the light and the soul receives that light. That light, if accepted, will bring peace to the soul.

I Need Balance

Within me lies a mystery that keeps me searching for clarity to the inner self of this existence called life. Daily, I ponder sometimes becoming lost in this never-ending, and at times relentless, struggle to find contentment. As I try to put together the pieces of the puzzle, my thoughts direct my attention to a scale. Ah! Balance! That is the key to my mystery. I need balance.

Knowing

I won't know God until I know myself; therefore, I will never know myself until I know God. Again it is not in my knowledge but in my knowing. Many have knowledge but few know. Ask Judas and Pharaoh. Do I truly know Him?

The Wisdom of a Fool

Oftentimes I find myself living to myself, because I am the only one who understands me, or so I think. But if truth be told, self could be deceiving me for selfish gain. How can that be? Am I that delusional? Am I too close to me to objectively draw such a conclusion? Being wrong may be too painful a pill to swallow. There is hidden pride within that hates to be wrong, so I must remain living a life of a fool.

Headed Down the Path to Nowhere

      Without a purpose, I am on that road.
Without a plan, I am determined to fall and fail. Without the drive, most assuredly I will wreck. Without the right mindset, life will have no meaning.
The road to nowhere is a road of darkness filled with pitfalls and potholes.
Without the light of Jesus shinning in and through me, I will cease to live, but merely exist.
"Thy Word is a lamp unto my feet, and a light to my path" (Psalm 119:105)

Hiding in the Crevices of Your Darkness

A denial of truth will harden the heart and result in seclusion and sinking deeper into the loss of reality, causing the opportunity of life to have no meaning.

The Peace Within

Now I lay me down to rest After I have tried to do my best. I may not succeed in every attempt, but by the Grace of God, I am content. Where does this peace within me lie?

It is the love of God in which I abide. (Philippians 4:7)

The Driving Force Behind the Scene

Encased in this frame (the body) dwells a being called the soul of man, the spirit of man. That which is inside, or behind the scene, causes an action or reaction that is outwardly manifested so the invisible can become visible. Pondering in the mind how complex but how wonderfully man is made reveals the awesomeness of the Creator.
"For in Him we live, move and have our being" (Acts 17:28).

Dormant

    I lay dormant, but I was planned. I lay dormant, but I was purposed. I lay dormant, but I had potential. I lay dormant, yet without power.
I lay dormant, yet not known but was foreknown. I lay dormant, without sight but soon to see.
Then the omnipotent, omnipresent, omniscient God breathed the breath of life in me, and I became a living soul.

Settling Down to Living

    The flower blooms but it also fades.
The trees fill their limbs with leaves, but they also bare their nakedness.
The water flows but also ebbs. The sun rises but also sets.
Morning turns to evening, which turns to night. Changes are constant.
Time matures.
Understanding of life strengthens the soul.
The appreciation of life replaces the uncertainty of life. I have settled down to living.

DID I FORGET TO SAY THANK YOU?

In my rush to the table, in my many activities of the day, did I forget to say thank you?
When I overslept and was in a rush to work, did I slow down and say thank you?
In the countless beats of my heart, did I forget to say, thank you?
Through the pain that sometimes I endure and the disappointments I sometimes have, did I forget to say thank you?
When at times in that state of confusion and even doubt, did I forget to say thank you? Even when the blessings came my way or when the blessings were denied, did I pause to say thank you?
I pause right now to say, "Thank you God, for being Lord of my life".

I Taught Someone Today

I don't have a degree in math, English, economics, or science. I am not employed at any educational institution, but I taught someone today. Aware or unaware of my actions, someone learned from me. Was I pleasing in the sight of God, or was He ashamed of me? I claim to be His child. I claim to be set apart for His Kingdom. The Word of God says that we must all appear before the judgment seat. I taught someone today. Was it good or bad?

I Must Do My Part

The promises of God are not without cost. I must do my part. He created the heavens and the earth and all that is therein just for me. But I must do my part. He also created me in His own image. I have to do my part. He even sent His Son (Himself) as an example, to live in a fleshly body like mine, to suffer, to die a shameful death, to be buried but to be resurrected with the declaration that all power is in His hand, to ascend to heaven, and to come back again. I have to do my part. For me to receive the power, protection, and provision that He has promised ("Lo, I am with you always, even to the end of the age"), I must be born again (John 3:16, Romans 10:9-10; Romans 12:2-5).

God of Grace, God of Mercy

When I find myself caught up in life's careless and reckless ways, there is grace and there is mercy. Even when there is danger seen and unseen, there is grace and there is mercy.
Never am I worthy, but there is grace and there is mercy. I praise God for His grace and His mercy.

The Omnipotence of God

Some of my deepest thoughts are my darkest, which can only remain hidden by the Spirit of God who dwells in me. Daily I must ask the saving grace of God to hide me behind the cross and keep me covered by the blood of Jesus. I am assured that His power will restrain and refrain that which is evil within me.
"Oh wretched man that I am! Who shall deliver me from the body of this death" (Romans 7:24)?

Deceived

Have I learned from my mistakes, or am I a repeat offender? I should heed the warning before I become a victim of my own trap. I have seen firsthand the results of the repeat offender. Have I learn from my mistakes, or have I become addicted by my own devices caused by deception?

I Got Dressed Today

I adorned myself with pride, prestige, and purity.
I also got dressed today, but I adorned myself with the whole armor of God (power, provision, protection, and also His promises).

Failure/Hope

The failure to succeed is the absence of not trying, the mindset not to continue to try, and the lost vision of hope, for hope is the constant expectation of an unseen reality.

Faith's Takeover

When the possible seems too impossible and the challenges too great, faith must take over. As the hurts begin to intensify and the problems multiply, faith must take over.

When all, I feel, has been done and there is still no resolve, faith must take over.

When time seems to be my worst enemy, then faith must take over.

All things are done in God's appointed time. It's my faith in which I depend. It's my faith in God that brings deliverance and peace. I have within my grasp the resolve for me. It's my faith through grace.

Awake

I was awakened this morning by the power of God. I started this day by the power of God. Things were not as I wanted them to be, but I found rest in the power of God. The trees agree with me because their leaves will soon turn brown and fall. They would love to remain green and in full bloom, but they understand their season. I rest in this season of mine, for I know that it's just a season. There will be the season when my leaves (fulfillment and prosperity) will return green by the power of God. So this day I will gain strength in my season.

The Need to Recall (The Reflection)

Early this morning as I sat in meditation, my eyes scanned the room, and I found myself looking at the comfort and peace that I possessed. My attention was not on what I needed or what I desired but at the moment a place of contentment. I then started to recall and reflect. I have been preserved (kept) by grace and mercy though many times at the crossroads of giving up and giving in, but at this moment, I am comforted.

Then I realized that I can look past yesterday and today and visualize tomorrow. My needs were met and some desires fulfilled. Now I have the confidence to look beyond the moment and reach for that which is yet to come. And so I look in hope for what can be and what shall come to pass. I thank God for my recollection.

Pruning

The pruning of trees helps the weakness they bear in order to stand tall against the storms that lie ahead. So it is of man who stands tall for the Gospel. Pruning is a way of proving one's faith, not only to oneself, but to the faithless who witness and even those who participate.

Completeness

At birth I was born of woman with the necessary features to grow from infancy to childhood, from childhood to adolescence and from teen age to adulthood. If God so allows at the apex of my life, I will begin to decline in strength and mobility. That is the process of life.

But I am incomplete and incapable of reaching that stage of completeness. At birth I was born with a defect called sin. Regardless of my achievements or non- achievements, within myself, I am unequipped and powerless to reach that stage. With limited knowledge, I was unaware of how infectious the disease was that was trying to eat away at my eternal soul. The physical imperfections that infiltrate my exterior and interior being are the results of a man called Adam, a perfect man. But because of God's love, He gave man freewill.

Adam chose to disobey, causing sin to be in the DNA of all mankind. It would take the sacrifice of God's only begotten to save man from a destined hell. Only when I believe and when my flesh dies can there be completeness.

Closer and Closer

When life began, man walked with God. The daily fellowship drew man closer and closer to Him. God rewarded man by giving him dominion over His creation. He even gave man the power to name all the animals. God even provided man a helpmate, woman. They walked closer together. But because of man's disobedience, man began to draw away instead of closer. God provided a way through His Son, but man continues to draw from Him and draw closer and closer to the world. The knowledge of man has increased, thereby driving man further from God and even closer to the world. God has a plan. His Son will return to gather those who stayed close to Him, leaving behind those who continue to withdraw to suffer unimaginable affliction. Draw closer to God, and He will draw closer to you.

New Year's Resolution

Soon to be the end of year 2017 and the beginning of 2018. How can this be so grand if today is a repeat of yesterday? Why even consider 2018 if I am still caught up in self-pride and self-pity, stuck in laziness and self containment? Should I just rewind the DVD, cassette, or tape recorder and know how the next year will be?
Or should I get a grip on my life and realize what a fool I have been and that nothing changes until I change and accept my inefficiencies and cry out for help?

Synthetic Religion

Freedom, as the world has so deemed, has launched and released a spirit of a slothful and a negative attitude into those who are struggling with self-identification and self-doubt whereby their minds have become imprisoned by Satan's tactics.

God's Presence

(I am before you were. I am while you are. I will be after you are).
I thought I was alone. The feeling was real, as though the inside of me was void and empty. Even to the point that the meals which I consumed left me still craving for more. I was still empty. In a crowd with the laughter and gaiety of the people, I felt isolated and deserted. No matter day or night, loneliness became my nature. But within me, somewhere, I wanted to feel alive. I lifted my head and gazed at the heavens. The light I saw was like none other. The warmth of the ray began to illuminate the outside of me then penetrated deep within my soul. A sound resounded through my ears: "You are never alone. I was yesterday, I am today, I am forevermore. I am omnipresent. I am God."

Who Is Controlling Me

Who is controlling me? A question asked which cannot easily be answered unless there is an accepted understanding of my mind. If I judge before I completely comprehend its fullness, I will, without a true foundation, respond unwisely. The Word of God is true and can never be changed to alter my decision. I am in control of me---that is, my mind---because I have been given free will by God. I may not be able to change my circumstances, but thinking positively or negatively is in my control. David says, "I will bless the Lord at all times, His praises shall continually be in my mouth." The words of control are I will and my mouth. I control myself.

Put to the Test

This morning as I sat reading and meditating, the words put to the test magnified themselves. God's Word was, is, and will always be truth only to those who are willing to be put to the test. I won't pass the test unless I am willing to take the test. I won't win until I realize that I may lose but am willing to be put to the test. We walk by faith, not by sight.

Change

Life is a moment-to-moment living interrupted by a second-to-second change. The foreknowledge when revealed will interfere with normality causing emotions to make an adjustment to the interruptions in life.

The Thin Line

How strong are the words I speak? What effect do my words have on those who hear and even what I hear? Are they words that will encourage or discourage? Will they build up or tear down? Will they badger or bless? Will they hinder or help, destroy or save? There is a thin line that divides right from wrong. Do I understand that life and death are in the tongue? My unbridled tongue is a lethal weapon that can commit and will commit murder. I must bridle my tongue.

Infinite

Infinite is a word that describes something that is indescribable, never changing, immeasurable, limitless, never-ending and incomprehensible. That sounds like the attributes of God. God is able to cast my sins as far as the east is from the west.

Smell the Dirt

Every now and then I fall down and smell the dirt. I should never think so highly of myself that I forget who I am. Through my success I will experience some failures to help in my remembrance of an imperfect creature. No one is immune to downfalls. I thank God for the falls, for He created us all from the dust of the earth.

Searching

Have you heard the song lyrics, "looking for love in all the wrong places"? The irony of those words is that love is not lost. The world was created because of love. Christ died out of love and because of love. Love is just a mirror glance away. I can't find love if at first I don't know that I am loved. I must first love myself. There is nothing I can do or no emotion I can feel, no matter how lost or alone I am, that the love of God can't comfort. It all begins with me and my inner search for love. (John 3:16)

Tomorrow

Adverb: on the day after today Noun: the day after today
Looking at the definitions, I find myself unknowingly ignoring my today and proceeding to live in an un-promised time. Yes, I must prepare, but tomorrow will never be, for today is tomorrow. I can never live past my present, because I am unaware of my nighttime. Matthew 6:34 tells me to take no thought of tomorrow, for sufficient is the day.

The Roads

There are only two roads in life. Regardless of who I am, I only have one to choose. The roads do not discriminate. They will not segregate. I may try to take both, but it would be impossible to do. They oppose each other. They go in different directions. They do have things in common. Both have hills and valleys, curves, rough places, caution signs, stormy weather, and even rest stops. I can achieve financial success. I can gain notoriety. Both roads have an ending. Both roads will end in eternity, eternity in hell or eternity in heaven. On the road to hell you will be swayed by Satan's lies and deceit. On the road to heaven, you will be guided by the Holy Spirit with grace and mercy. Which road am I on?

The Body

"Take care of your body. It is the only place you have to live." I saw this sign in my dentist's office and wondered whether those who read it understood it. The reality of the statement is that there is a living soul within, a being, embodied within the frame of the body. Our natural eye cannot see the wind, only the effect.

Far greater is the spirit that is within. Only spirit can see spirit. Our natural sight can only see the natural. Our physical sight was designed by God to allow the beauty of creation to be seen and enjoyed. But most of all, our physical nature was created so that we can choose (free will).

Pressing Forward

Paul writes, "I press toward the mark for the prize of the high call of God in Christ Jesus" (Philippians 3:14). What is Paul saying? I thrust in the direction of something worth striving for, a highly desirable surge toward a particular way of life expressed in the relationship between a direction and a point of reference by Jehovah through His Son!

I Am Who I Am

      I am who I am because I have labored in my efforts.
If I am an egotist, I have labored relentlessly to master the image.
If I am lazy and inconsiderate, then I sanction the action through my labor.
If I love and I share, my focus is to achieve that which embodies loving and sharing.
If I focus on my failures and shift the blame, I become who I am, a failure.
If I am down but seriously desire to get up, I will reach upward regardless of how low I get.
I learn how to master who I am.

Emotional, Not Spiritual

Emotionally excited, but spiritually dormant: the fate of those going through life's woes, yet never gaining spiritual strength. Externally they pretend to be living in the blessings of God, but are internally void of peace and joy.

Miracle

I don't have to open a Bible to read about a miracle. All I have to do is look in the mirror. In case there are no mirrors around, all I have to do is touch myself, and I will feel a miracle. The greatest miracle ever is in knowing the fact that I am a miracle.

Perfection

God had a perfect purpose. God has a perfect purpose. In the beginning God created a perfect purpose. Everything great, everything small had/has a perfect purpose. Everything good and everything evil had/has a perfect purpose. I can't understand it, nor can I describe it.

Sight

How do I see? What do I see? Where does it originate? Why do I see what I see? How can I internalize and draw the conclusion that what I see is real or accurate or true? I am reminded of Eve in the Garden of Eden. She first heard, then saw, then acted upon what she saw, or was it what she saw, then heard? Persecutor Saul, in his relentless zeal toward the persecution of the Jews, either in his eyes saw and his heart felt rightness in his action or the heart determined what his eyes saw. Does my sight come from the eyes I look through or from the soul, within which lies the seat of my emotions? When I meditate and seek God's Word, I must go past my natural and search deeper as I study. Paul had sight to see but was blinded to truth. He was blinded in sight but received spiritual sight.
His eyes were opened to see what he could not see. How do I see?

My World

If I only see or experience God moving and doing great things only on Sunday, then I have placed Him in a box and I lowered myself to an event. If I cannot see the move of God with every breath and every step I take and make, I have lowered the voltage of His power and diminished His sovereignty. If my life only revolves around my family, I cease to see the Great Commission, and my witness becomes self- centered, my direction self-consumed, my purpose self- contained, my growth stunted, my deliverance dwindled, my joy, my peace, and my contentment lost in a selfish, clannish world because I have forgotten that the "earth is the Lord's, and the fullness thereof, and they that dwell therein." I've got to get out of my world and step into God's world!

Tomorrow

Tomorrow is the distant that appears to be in the grasp of reality but is so far away that it can never be attained. For tomorrow can never be. Tomorrow is today. I have the moment, the second. Only as time allows me to see, and feel can I live.

The Cross

In His infinite wisdom, His sovereignty and love placed mankind on an even playing field. There are rich and poor, short and tall. Some are handsome and beautiful. Some are physically fit, and some are physically challenged. There are different ethnicities. There are those with great minds, strength, and power and those with lesser capabilities. Some have great, little, or very limited talent. No matter who we are, the common denominator is the same, the cross. It is at the cross where we win or lose. Winners will have eternal life in heaven with the Creator, and losers, eternal life in hell. Our status has no power.

Salvation

     Salvation is not an event but a converted growth. I liken it to birth. I don't remember the moment when I was conceived or when I left my mother's womb. I don't remember my first step or my first word. What was the first thing I saw? I didn't realize that I was alive. But as I grew, life became more visible. The voice of mother and the touch of mother became clearer.

As I began to grow, the nurturing of mother, through the infinite wisdom of God Almighty, opened the door to the knowledge of my existence.

Events have a set day. Conversion is daily. Praying is daily. Praising is daily. Loving and forgiving and surrendering are daily. Do you/I know the day or hour or place? All I need to know is that I'm not like I used to be and that I'm trying to be more like Him each day. I do know without a shadow of doubt that I shall see Him one day face-to-face. That is my hope.

That is my desire. I wait with anticipation. Do not limit salvation to only an event (day, time, or place).

A child of the King

Twilight of Confusion

Twilight: described as half-light, semi dark, gloom; the paradoxical state of mind with the uncertainty of purpose and direction.
In a world with avenues that can aid in the search for self worth, a world of modern technology where just one touch of a finger can open doors to unlimited opportunities, why do many still live in a twilight of confusion? They refuse to accept the Light of the World. John 8:12.

Is God Pleased With Me?

If I take a true and accurate assessment of myself, can I with accuracy say yes?
Regardless of the world around me, the ups and downs, setbacks, disappointments, success, or anything pertaining to my existence, will the answer be yes?
However high or low I am in the eyes of man, there is but one who ultimately will say, "This is my child in whom I am well pleased." I can't get it twisted by the wiles of Satan. Humble me, God, as I go down into the water, and when I rise up, let heaven open up and Your voice speak to me. "This is my son in who I am well pleased."

For Those Who Have No Hope

Hope, the constant expectation of an unseen reality. When does it end? When does the search end for the things desired? It ends when I cease to pursue. Far greater is the opportunity to achieve when the mind controls the circumstances than when the circumstances control the mind. Limits come and place doubt when sights are in only what we see. The Word of God teaches that eyes have not seen nor ears heard!

It is Personal

Psalm 139:14 I will praise thee; I am fearfully and wonderfully made: marvelous are thy works; and that my soul knoweth right well. Until I forget the religious hype, the church clichés, the dressed-up prayers and the unfounded praise, the crowd-pleasing songs and scripted analytical sermons, I will never appreciate the value of my creator. I was handmade, fashioned by His hand. His breath gave me life.

Who I am is because of who He is. He took pride in forming me and shaping me to the point of being created in His own image. The cost for my birth was the death of His Son. What a price to pay. I must bare myself before Him. Why should I lower my standard of worship to please man? I praise the one who can do all things but fail because He takes care of me personally. I don't need the hype.

If

This may be one of the most powerful words in all the English vocabulary. Or is this the most powerful word in life? When used as a noun, if means "a condition or supposition." When I concentrate on this word, I must surely be accurate in my conclusion. The end results of that concentration could end in success or failure, life or death, sickness or health, good or bad. The most important conclusion is that it could mean eternal life in heaven or in hell. To thy own self be true.

Life's Setbacks

At the very moment of deliverance, I was dealt a setback.
At the very moment of elevation, there was a tugging force trying to pull me back down. At the very moment that I could see the sunshine, there came a dark cloud. At the very moment that peace and joy had surrounded me, there came an army of pain and sorrow. Becoming perplexed, I had to call to memory the one I trust through scripture: Psalm 34:19 (Many are the afflictions of the righteous"), Romans 8:28, and 2 Corinthians 4:13-18. I pray the days ahead are fruitful as you walk in the divine calling of God. Never let your guard down. Be aware of your surroundings and those you surround yourself with.

You Wear It Well

When bathed in the presence of God, the cares of this world are hidden behind the cross. Though life will happen because the Word is true, it rains on the just as well as the unjust, but the presence of God is a shelter and fortress for you. You wear it well against the disappointments and the woes of life, for you trust in Him. Tears are common to everyone. Sorrow will find you. Death has surrounded you. Satan will stalk you. Sin will tempt you. But you wear it well, the presence of God that controls you. (Ephesians 6:10-18)

The Hidden Things of God

Be not deceived. The Word of God is true. It is truth. What I believe and what I think can be deceiving if I'm not willing to search my heart, release my mind, and ask God to reveal truth by His Holy Spirit. I must be willing to put aside what I have heard, what I have been taught, and what I feel is true. Since God created me, I must depend on my faith and surrender my mind, body, and soul to Him. Revelation of truth will come when I surrender my all to Him. His Word will confound the mind of the wise but give clarity to the meek. I hunger and thirst for righteousness. For God I live. For God I die.

When "I" Become Bigger Than Me

Paradoxically speaking, what an outlandish thought! Though seemingly impossible, the realism is very prevalent and true. Examining the thought behind the statement, I find the hidden answer to what appears to be an absurd statement. Webster describes I as "self or ego". Ego by definition is that driving force that can cause one to think more highly of oneself than he should, therefore causing I to become bigger than me. I remain humble when the Bible reminds me of God's Word: Matthew 5:5, 1 Corinthians 15:9; Philippians 3:8.

The World

The place that God created for the inhabitance of His people for the purpose of the sharing of His Kingdom on earth as it is in heaven. His love was so tremendous that He gave/gives all an opportunity to partake of the splendor of His glory.

Death

Death is private. Death is personal.
Death of this body is permanent. Don't take it likely.
Everyone is a participant. Likewise, eternity is private.
Eternity is personal.
Eternity is permanent.
Everyone will participate in either heaven or hell.
To hear the conclusion, life, death, and eternity are real.
Where will your residency be?

Power

Never should one underestimate the power of believing and knowing. When the mind is convinced and the heart is convicted, believing becomes the driving force in knowing.

Revelation

Bible revelation is revealed through life's application. If the Bible is read as a book, we will only see characters. If the Bible is studied to reveal its purpose for our lives, we will, through seeking knowledge from God, live in accordance to His divine will and divine purpose.

Alone in a Crowd

There is a world outside of me that is revealed. I can see lights, the hustle and the bustle of millions. I can hear the sounds of laughter, the sound of music. I can see the tears of happiness, also the tears of sorrow. Despite what I see and hear, I feel alone in a crowd. There is a world within that is hidden from view. The secret beds of thoughts and feelings are privy to me only. Should I choose, I may unveil only that which pleases me and that which I feel I control. I live in a crowd but also alone in the crowd.

I Must Finish Well

I must finish well that which has been placed before me even before the foundation of this world. I must finish well the predestination of my salvation. I must finish well this Christian race. I must finish well in the mist of the diversities of distractions. I must finish well to claim the promise---that promise as I cross the finish line: "Be thou faithful unto death, and I will give thee a crown of life" (Revelation 2:10). For no man, having put his hand to the plow, and looking back, is fit for the service in the Kingdom of the Lord" (Luke 9:62).
I must finish well.

Mother

The second Sunday of May is the day set aside to honor mothers. I appreciate and honor the deed, but it lacks in fulfillment. Gifts are given, dinners are prepared and recognition expressed in appreciation. But I honor you this day not with gifts or mere words, but I honor you every day for your steadfastness, your unrelenting desire to fulfill the principles of a virtuous woman created by God, who inspires you by the power of His Holy Spirit to love unconditionally and to look for greatness in mankind as only a mother can. You are the epitome in my mind and my heart of a mother. I praise God for the mother of my children.

I Choose

I am an asset or I am a liability
I am either productive or nonproductive. I am moving forward or standing still.
I am either growing or stagnant.
I have the ability within to achieve through the help of God, who created me.
I make the choice. I choose.
The mind (soul) reveals choices (free will). Choices (options) give way to decisions. Decisions are the end result of how we choose.

Steady

There are far too many who live their Christian life in segments instead of living in continuance. When life happens, they become unsure and insecure. Their faith wavers and commitment lessens. Participation becomes part-time, and obedience is sometimes. Prayer and praise is hidden in self pity and adolescent pouting. Going through becomes the norm and fault-finding the language.

It's On Me

It's not on God. It's not on man. It's on me.
That which I need has already been provided. Even those desires that I have, if it is to make me better and bring Him glory, will be. If I desire a deeper knowledge of Him, He will provide. It is when in sorrow, trouble, doubt, and fear will He give me peace, joy, and strength. Most assuredly when I err in sin will He with open arms receive me back if my heart repents and my mind turns back to Him. It's on me to obey. His Word says, "I stand at the door and knock." He will enter only if I am willing to open the door and invite Him in. No one can do it but me. I may try and shift responsibilities on others, but it's on me.

Decision

That space in time between thought and action is decision.
Impulse action can negate a choice, which could result in a lifetime of regret. What I choose is in the weighing of or the comparing of the choices I have, which is ultimately in my control. I cannot control the results, but I can control my decisions.

No Man Is an Island

How can I look around and see the flowers bloom, the trees sway in the breeze, the rivers flow, the snow covers the mountaintops, the rain falls, nature drink, and the laughter, the tears shed, the joy and peace in others, when there is so much misery, so much loneliness, so many needy in the world of plenty? Am I that caught up, self-absorbed, attending my own pity party, in a denial state, doubting mindset that nobody cares and nobody understands me in my state of mind that I have lost sight of who created all? Lord, forgive me.

Life

How do I face life? Where do I go for the answer? Am I in search of truth or in search of that which would appease my natural feelings? Does the fear of reality cause me to cover up, or am I strong enough to take it? The question may be, where does my strength lie? I must realize that I am but an earthen vessel molded and shaped in human form, which dissolves daily. The potter who created me is my answer to life.
Matthew 10:28 is my answer.

Miracles

In searching for answers that will bring peace, I'm reminded of those miracles Jesus preformed. They reveal the power of an awesome God. Even raising the dead is unexplainable. There were/are a multitude of miracles which were and are performed. I believe the greatest of all is the forgiveness of sin by confession of sinful creatures. The greatest miracle is the new birth, and after this mortal has put on immortality, that is when I will be just like Him. That is an everlasting miracle.

My Birth

Little did I know that my birth would be so grand, because in the early stages of my life someone had to feed me, not only the nourishing of my body so that I could grow physically, but there was someone there also who fed my soul so that I would be completed. The steps I took when I realized I could walk on my own carried me through many years of choices, some good and some bad. That foundation at the beginning of life carried me to the years where I had to apply that which had been in me. When I was a child, I spoke as a child, I understood as a child, I thought as a child: But when I became a man, I put away childish things.

I

I was created to live. I was made to die so that I could live. To understand this, I must first believe and accept and know that God is God. What I see in the natural is only an image of who I am. I am a moth caterpillar which must be transformed/must metamorphose into a beautiful (butterfly) soul saved by grace through redemption.

A World of Plenty

The world, this universe, was brought into existence by "let there be" and "let us." The world, this universe, supplies the needs of its inhabitants. Nothing would be added because of the omniscience of the one who created it. This world, this universe, was given to the inhabitants to show the omnipotence of the Creator. I was not left alone but am continuously watched by the omnipresence of He who controls that which was created. As I observe and as I look out and see pestilence, envy, the disregard for lives which inhabits this world, I ask the question, how can this be? The words come to mind: "Be not dismayed whate'er betide, God will take care of you.
Beneath His wings of love abide, God will take care of you."

Breaking News

There is a spiritual war that is being fought between God and Satan, not between the color of man and the superiority of man. The war is between good and evil. But don't be alarmed, because the battle has already been won. Are you on the winning side?

Preparation

Am I in the process of making ready in advance that which is inevitable, unavoidable, or inescapable? Am I so lost in the living that I have forgotten to live? Has my focus been diverted to the now forgetting that which is to come? Am I so involved in the temporal things of life that I forget or forgotten that there is a life after living? There are so many questions that I have not answered because of the obscurity or lack of concern. Regardless of how I think or feel, if preparation is not made today, today could be my last day. I have no control over tomorrow, for today is the day of salvation. Have I made preparation for what is to come? Am I prepared?

Signed, My soul

Example Is the Best Precept

I often comment on the mannerisms of others sometimes unjustifiable. Even if it is true, am I justified or even qualified? Have I taken a walk around my life and recorded from head to toe every imperfection in me? The image that I view in the mirror will always bare truths, but do I accept? I am afraid that I have gone past my right to spotlight. My plate is too full correcting myself.

Open Eyes

I just experienced a spiritual revelation. Some would say that I am physically fit, am young for my age, look good in clothes, but little do they know that I have backslid and am in bad shape. My stamina and strength is weak. Why? Because I have taken a break from what has brought me this far.

Looks can be deceiving. Sounds like this Christian walk. Saved but spiritually weak. Why? Little or no prayer. No meditation and daily study of the Word. No fellowship with other believers. Know-it-all in the mind but deficient in faith. Not willing to be taught. Believe they are blessed and highly favored but in essence highly faulty. Why? Because they have taken a spiritual break.

You're Choice

"You get the one you pick in a relationship, not a Prince Charming," quoted a judge on a TV show. A rose is a rose. A fool is a fool. Right is right, wrong is wrong. If you eat a lemon, prepare for a sour taste. A leopard can be painted, but you can't change his spots.

GOD HAD A PERFECT PURPOSE

God has a perfect purpose!
In the beginning God created a perfect purpose.
Everything great, everything small had/has a perfect purpose. Everything good, everything evil had/has a perfect purpose. I can't understand it, nor can I describe it.
If I live a life of excuses, I will always hide the truth.

Defeated Yet Victorious

With every breath I take, it is done so in defeat or victory.
The more I am defeated, the more I am victorious. I have, must have a willing attitude to be defeated so that I can be victorious. This sounds like an oxymoron but in reality it is one who has been transformed to a new way of life. Every day and with every step I take, I "must" pray for, live and shout for defeat. The question I must ask myself, do I truly want to be victorious? My eternal existence hinges on my answer. There can be no balancing act to even the scale. I want either to be defeated in order to be victorious or I will ultimately be defeated. I must die daily.

The Breath of God

Separating myself from the rush in life to the serenity and peace which God can give to all, I cannot help but to pause in humility at the divine power of my creator. I (Adam/man) was created, shaped and formed by the hands of God from the dust of the earth. He blew into my nostrils the breath of life causing me to come alive. His breath gave me the power to think and a voice to talk and legs to walk. That breath also gave me the ability to grow, to reason, to cry and to laugh. Just His breath was enough to do what He had designed for me. I glory in His breath.

A Trip or Journey

Am I on a trip or journey?
Trip-an act of going to a place and returning Journey--an act of `going from one place to another How many times have I been taking trips only to return to despair, hurt, rejection and loneliness? My plight will always be like a maze if I have no direction or refuse to accept change. I need to be on life's journey. I need to be on that journey which will take me from failure to success, from hurting to healing, from incomplete to complete.

My Daily Living

Let the words of my mouth (that which is released from my lips to be heard) and the meditation of my heart (the truth and the witness of emotions, feelings and desires) be acceptable (approved, morally sound, pure and untainted) in thou sight (omnipotent, omnipresent, omniscient God), O Lord (supreme, sovereign, ruler of heaven and earth) my strength (source of life, solid rock, firm foundation) and my redeemer (Christ the risen King).

Taking the Strength Test

    Be sure of your strength. Take the test. I will never know how much weight I can lift until I pick it up. The more times I lift, the stronger I become and heavier weights will I be able to lift. Assumptions are destroying the spiritual image of Christians because of the unwillingness to test their strength.
Until you bear the burden you will never know how heavy the load. Until you have a desire to pick up that load (the cross) to test your faith, you will remain weak even though you think you are strong. There is a cross we all must bear because of the one who saves, Jesus Christ, carried all sins to the old rugged cross and was lifted high with the sins of the world on His shoulders. We too must carry our load.
Matthew 16:23-25

Burger King

I wish I were Burger King, then, I could have it my way. I would order life the way that would please me. I would order it without onions because it would leave a bad taste in my mouth (discipline). Or just because I like them, I would add extra and wouldn't worry whether my breath was offensive or not (self-centered). Aah, French fries. A double whopper please! Add more salt. Two, no make that three slices of cheese. Give me an extra-large drink. I think for supper I'll have a triple whopper (abusing the temple of God). I'd better stop at the store and get some anti-acid. Better pick up some sleep aid. I won't be able to sleep with all that in my stomach (camouflaging a wrong). Who cares? I want it my way because I am Burger King (unfeeling). Why am I dreaming? If I have it my way, I would lose my way.

My Focus

Looking for a profound definition for focus, my attention was drawn to the word "Cornerstone". Cornerstone: that which holds and shapes the foundation, the strength of the house. Cornerstone is that perfect beginning that brings a positive end. So my focus should be that of a cornerstone which would shape me morally and spiritually into a strong believer in the one who is the "chief cornerstone", Jesus Christ.

Challenged

    Each day I am challenged to live a fulfilled and faithful life.
Taking advantage of the sand that remains in my hour glass will keep my mind and thought from frolicking in foolish maneuvers that would not produce a fruitful pebble of sand. Just one pebble, breath, delinquently abused and dropped is lost and can never be replaced.

www.ingramcontent.com/pod-product-compliance
Lightning Source LLC
Chambersburg PA
CBHW030157100526
44592CB00009B/321